BLOSSOM

A BOOK OF POEMS

RAISUN MATHEW

Made with ♥ on the Notion Press Platform
www.notionpress.com

*

2022-2026
Information Science and Engineering
Computer Science and Engineering (General: Section C)

Jain (Deemed-to-be University)
Bangalore, Karnataka, India

*

Contents

Contents

Preface

Every bloom has a past that is unnoticed or ignored by those who wish to focus only on its successful blossom. The series of unsuccessful attempts and unwelcome failures are usually ignored, but they always exist to become the untold personal stories of the flower. In a world that goes behind success, the sweet bitterness of the long list may be one among many similar experiences. However, the difficulties associated with a successful attempt to bloom from a bud earn respect, value, and integrity. The life of a successful engineer is similar to that of a beautiful flower that had to wait for its chance to bloom by surpassing several obstacles on the way to the ultimate dream.

Life can be cruel at times, taking on the role of an antagonist. However, as we have to be the protagonist in the play written by the unseen playwright who defines and describes the scenes, it is necessary to fight until the moment of blossom. The pain of pretending to be the protagonist, the thorns of acting as if nothing has hurt, and the torment of becoming normal even in uncertain situations make it the right way for an artistic performer to live in a world that is loaded with unreal existences and notions about life.

As William Shakespeare wrote, "To be, or not to be, that is the question." It is not a fault to make mistakes, but it is a fault not to begin to chase your passion due to the fear of making mistakes. Students of Information Science and Engineering (ISE) and Computer Science and Engineering (General: Section - C), batch of 2022-26 at Jain (Deemed-to-be University), Bangalore, have used their creativity to open the door to the freedom of thinking about the future, remembering the past, and experiencing the present.

Dr. Raisun Mathew
Assistant Professor of English
Jain (Deemed-to-be University)
Bangalore, Karnataka, India

Acknowledgements

Sincere thanks to,

Notion Press

*

Faculty of Engineering and Technology
Jain (Deemed-to-be University)
Bangalore, Karnataka, India

1

I Dumped My Heart!

- SOHAN M. -

****

It broke me from inside,
But kept me joined outside
I wanted to hate it forever,
And not talk it ever
It hit me on my soul like dart
So I decided to dump my heart!

It ditched me every day n night,
And we ended up in or fight
I cried and I screamed aloud,
But the pain didn't go out
It made me live so hard,
So I decided to dump my heart!

It made me feel helpless,
Without me, I felt so useless
There was nothing more left in heart
And laughed out aloud when I fell
There was nothing more left in heart
So I decided to dump my heart!

2

Did She Ever?

- **HRISHITA NAYAK** -

****

You tell her you love her
You tell her she's enough
Oh, but how you treat her
Says something else.
You give her the freedom
With all her limitations
She tells you she's right
You tell her she was never
What are you trying to prove?
Her weakness or her fears
She never really got to know you
You made her vulnerable.
She is greater than all her fears
More than any of your definitions
She doesn't need you
Neither did she ever.

3

Gratitude

- PREM HOSURE -

****

If we were happy with what we had.
You make someone worry about anti-ageing.

Making them worry about everything,
You reflect on their weakness.

The peaceful lies or the painful truth
Both or neither,
You must welcome them gracefully.

We can feel the breeze of God
That exists on his planet,
And melt into his core unconditionally.

Get divine
Let all go where they belong to
GRATITUDE!

4

The Blame

- K. P. Sai Siri -

****

Another senseless death
God takes the blame

A young girl is stabbed
Left to bleed and die
In the arms of her love.

While many curse His name
A Furious bomb explodes
And God takes the blame

Innocents are left to die
As villains take pride
Beaming in their glory

While heartaches curse His name
The drunkard walks away
And God takes the blame

Life in a tangled heap

Slips away lost
As a sober drunkard enquires
The loved ones leave behind and
Sadly curse His name
"So much loss and tragedy."

While God takes the blame
People instantly cry out
"Why have you let this happen?"

As their hearts begin to doubt
Sadly the true villain walks
While many curses His name
Not realising the truth that

God takes all the blame.

5

I'm Done

- **KOTA PRANATI** -

****

I'm done fighting for causes long lost
I'm done trying to figure out what to do
I'm done doing my best to keep things up
I'm done sacrificing myself for your sake.

Mostly and mainly,
I'm done loving a romanticised idea of you
Because let's be honest
That person never existed in the first place.

6

The Dream

- **SAURABH KUMAR YADAV** -

****

Once, I had a dream
Where I dreamt about my dreams
While watching the television.

The dream of mine was so real
So-see through my surreal
That it took away all doubts
I had about my chances in life.

I saw myself as the dream
In the fantasy of mine.

Now that I face the real life
I see the probabilities
The dream is still alive
The surreal dream is my life

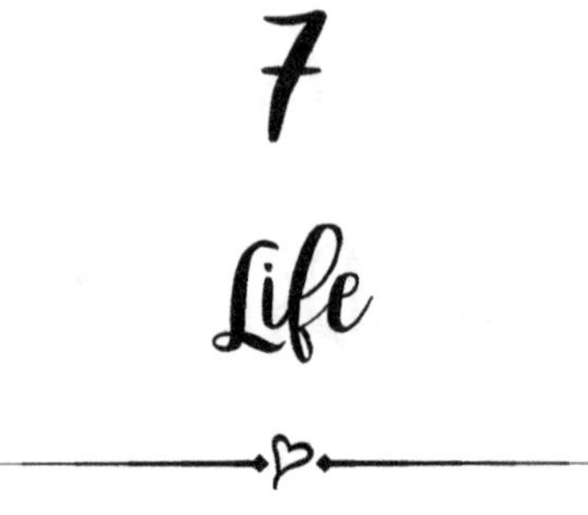

7 Life

- **MAHESH KUMAR PATI** -

****

Live the life you love
Love the life you live
For it is very short
And can never be bought.

Life can be good
Or it can be bad
You've gotten many things
You wish you never had.

Life is for enjoyment
Live yours to the fullest
For it is very short
And can never be bought.

Striving for big riches
Maybe a waste of time
Make the best of what you have
While you're still in your prime.

You've gotten many things
You wish you never had
Life is made for living
Whether it's happy or sad.

8

Cage in Life or Life in Cage

- **RAHUL RAJ** -

****

Like a little singing bird
In a golden cage
She sat there on ave.
Her voice. Oh, what a heavenly sound!
Got quieter by the day.

In the end
With nothing left
She shook her head,
Breakthrough
The wizard's magic.

That's when she realised
She was a prisoner
In a golden cage
With the door wide open
Behind her.

She was just too afraid
To leave the safety

Even though it meant
Being looked inside.
But from her fear
She rose and saved herself.

9

Lost Souls

- SHREEHARI MANU -

****

To all those kids who never returned for their dinner
To all those teachers who never returned to their children
In the name of the crucified, they still breathe
But all we go down is like bloody Mary,
Just another troubled kid I supposed
Or his dad who never believed
To the place where we were supposed to worship
Becomes a place where we sacrifice
To what we supposed to be another day
Was never meant to be our last day
Misery among the dreaded,
Countless lives pleaded
In a click, we become our memories,
Agony is all left for the loved ones,
For what is made for us is what kills us
Used in wars but is still among us
So all that I have seen now I ask them,
Why do we still have our rotten luck near us?

10

My Self

- ADITYA A. S. -

****

I think sometimes,
Why do I think so much
I cry sometimes
Trying to hide feelings as such

I doubt sometimes
Do I deserve this much?
Looking at the mirror
Into my eyes
I've got to do still much.

I think sometimes,
Why do I think so much?
I cry sometimes
Trying to hide feelings as such

I see God in the skies
Moon and stars as a stitch
Things nature has gifted us
I hope everyone gets to live as such

I think sometimes,
Why do I think so much?
I cry sometimes
Trying to hide feelings as such

11

Friends

- **MANSHI MISHRA** -

****

I stood all alone in the way,
Then came lots of people, and a lot of them walked away.

But a very few who remained at that time,
Are the people whom I call as mine.

They won't miss a chance to embarrass me,
But then won't let go off the ones who harass me.
They are the ones who destroy my fears,
They are the ones who wipe off my tears.

Running barefoot over the grasses,
To attending and bunking a few classes.
Fighting all day long like little kids,
Then enjoying in the rain with laughter and skids.

Ever ready to elope with me at times,
And always there to support me every time.
Being far away from my home,
Not even for a moment with them I ever felt alone.

Amongst us lies no conditions and no formalities,
Just a little bit of our tantrums and throwing off some royalties,
Even after having the worst strifes,
Those Idiots are the best part of my life.

12

Flying Times

- SHANTANU RAJ -

****

The light dims and the light glows
Wonderful and worst days
Comes and goes off
But life goes on with its show.

"LIFE" is a sweetheart
But turns up to make a great big mess
The way we go and come,
Problems say 'Hi' to us.

Sometimes, the mind lays something
And once the heart says something,
Mesmerising old days give us pleasure.

We cry, we smile
We fall and get up
Want to do something but alter it gradually
Doing anything other than the desired.

Life is nothing but just the presence of your body

Presence of many decisions
But lack of ignited minds
Not knowing what to do
But still in the air with
The sweet and salty flying times.

13

Lost and Never Found

- BHOOMIKA H. K. -

****

Standing still in the nothingness
Of the dark world
Fading in the thickness
Of the absurd.

Life falling down
Into pieces
Tears rolling down
For unknown reasons.

It's over now
Though not in my mind,
I still hear the sounds
Of my past and trauma combined.

I am dying, to be found
I am crying, to be heard
Not when I am six feet under the ground
Finally leaving behind the crowd.

14

The Endless Cycle

- AADITH NIDI -

****

I sit alone, observing everyone;
Tied-up with their lives; their phones.
Faces directed downwards, emotions seen
But only through the screens.
Chuckling, mourning, and raging all expressed
With a dead blank face.

They discern the real world to document inside a piece of metal,
Of others, of themselves, unaware of what's around them,
They roam with their eyes fixed on it.
A black and white life only seen vibrant through an empty box;
Unemptied as they are caged inside.

Unable to decipher what reality is,
Valuing the colourful people inside more
Than the ones in their dull world.
All of this is an endless cycle but the world keeps spinning;
Doesn't end, it stays the same but there's less in it.

15

Diary

- **SAILEJA SAHU** -

****

They call me their friend,
Talk to me about their day,
From start to end.

They talk to me when completely feeling blue,
Yes, I've heard a lot about you!

I've heard their cry,
When they had no one by their side,

They parted their loneliness with me,
When had no one to confide in.
I know their moods,
How they feel, happy, content or sad,
I've got to know enough about them,
All their qualities, good or bad.

But it's been a long time
Since they've been away,
Seems like they've got

No more words to say.

I choose to stay, hoping to hear
From them soon,
Maybe they've got a new friend,
Or they've started talking to the moon.

I realise maybe they are busy,
And don't need me anymore,
Anyways, I'm just a diary,
Who was once their best friend before.

16

Adam's Ale

- INCHARA S. -

****

I'm everywhere
You can see me anywhere.
I'll be staying in the pool,
Always looking very cool!

I will reach earth as the rain,
And is liked by every man.
Rain will turn to snow,
Later sunshine makes me flow!

You can see me in three states,
Solid, gas and liquid make my gait.
You can freeze me, warm me, boil me,
A day will not start without me!

I'll gallop like the tiger,
I have been called dead plants' driver.
I have a big cycle,
You can find me even as a spiral!

I'm clasped in a big barrage,
I can even make your mirage.
Even you will bring me fever,
Which puts me and you in danger!

I'm also present in the chapter,
People know water is the main factor.

17

Puzzled Peace

- NIKHIL REDDY K. -

- NIKHIL REDDY K. -

****

War to obtain peace
Failed and exhausted,
Tired and depressed,
Till we found it was just a dream
A waste of time, sacrifice and effort.

The selfish desire of craving peace
Causes wars and hatred is born to protect love,
The objective is to preserve peace and usher in war.

But I believe that someday,
The day will come when
People can truly understand each other.

But to that sometimes I feel,
The only things that exist in this world
Are pain and vanity.

18

Sweetheart

- SREERAM E. S. -

****

The day I met you is the most lovely day of my life
The moments we spend are the sweetest of my life
The time we enjoyed together is the most beautiful hours of my life
You are my everything, my sunshine, and my life!

Without you, my life is empty
Without you, I wish not to live in this world
You are the most precious gift I have ever received in my life.

All our pains and worries will drain one day
People against us will stand for us.

With you, I am happy and the luckiest man on the earth
Even death can't stop our precious love.
A day will come when the world would see
Our love and sacrifices!

19

The Invisible Me

- **SHREYA K.** -

****

How could they judge me by my appearance?
They didn't even talk to me once,
But bullying me for my appearance
Which lost my confidence at once.

They don't realise how their words hurt me
They bully me for fun, but it isn't fun for me.
They called me funny names, and expect me to help them.
I wish I could disappear at once.
I wish I dared to stand up for myself
But their words made me feel insecure about myself.
No one even noticed when I was in pain
Only my pillow knows my pain.

I wish I had a normal teenage
With a small group of friends to make memories.
I just want the world to accept me the way I am,
To be nice and kind to everyone.

20

LIFE - A Beautiful Journey

- RAKSHIT JAIN -

****

Life is so easy
Don't make it tough.
Sit take a sip of tea
And don't bother much.

Problems are for today, not tomorrow,
But mentos is forever, just have it once!

What is yours today
Will belong to someone else's tomorrow
Just go with the flow and explore a little bit.
As scars of experience are forever,
Which makes you beautiful every single hour.

No matter life is short just keep yourself in a nice way,
But don't forget your delicate heart.
Life is too simple don't make it complicated,
Sit take a sip of tea and don't bother much.

21
Hereafter

- S. RENGANAYAKI -

****

A dark thunderbolt hits suddenly!
The vessel slowly touches the cold blue water
Stormy threw everything towards him.
He turned around to see
The pitch dark room with none around.

With the feeling of slipping from reality
He questioned if there was really someone
Looking around, he blankly stares
At all lonely stars that shine along with the moon
Despite all the darkness around them.

Confused, he finally decided to sail.
Face them instead of running away
With a heart filled with anxiety and fear
Still believing in the universe
Only for his fate to be dark hereafter.

22

Dreams

- NEELURI PUNARVIKA -

****

A head full of dreams
I see the crystal vision of myself gleam
I can see the change I want to be
You got to lose to know how to achieve.

I lay awake at night and pray
Not to see the light of day
I wonder how to behave right
My mind can't get some respite.

Everybody got thin days in life to pay
Working hard for dreams to stay
We got to keep the fire burning, we gotta keep dreaming.
Hold your head up, and keep moving.

I don't care what the future brings, I would be fine
It is time to be taken to the front line
Gotta take a stance cause I won't get a second chance
It's a war which I need to make alone.

23

The Final Straw

- **AKSHARA AVASTHI** -

****

She wakes up an hour before the alarm goes off
For he has to be on time for work
She cooks silently, without letting out a cough
For her consort is the last person she'd want to irk.

She adjusts her wedding band, awaiting his arrival
"It'll be different today", is what she aspires
Her face lights up when she notices he's reading the Bible
Because when he's close to god, he doesn't add bruises to her attire

He leaves for work with a smile on his face
She is merry as she's proved her friends wrong. He's changed!
So she preps for a feast and gets fresh flowers for her vase
For love is blossoming in the union her parents had arranged.

When the clock hits six, she's all dolled up and
Done with cooking the meat
As her swain is about to return and ring the doorbell
But as soon as she opens the door, he knocks her off her feet
He screams, "Why are you dressed up like an escort Michelle?"

She knows she has made him mad again
As she hears the sound of her dishes break
And when she walks over to the kitchen to get some ice,
He's already left!
She murmurs to herself, "That bruise was healing, Jake."
Only this time, she is sure it's time for his arrest.

24

Waiting for Love

- FENIL GAJERA -

****

Stranded, all over
Hungry for love.
Feeling lower,
Villain, some unlove.

I'm a fire gone wild,
Burning like hell.
Broken inside,
As, all efforts fail.

I'm broken inside frozen,
And still, covered in white.
Fears are dozen,
As darkness steals the light.

But as long as wrong feels right,
I will never cry.
I be waiting for love, from the day to the night,
Never give up, I just try.

Night, approaching like a creep,
My horror screams.
Love, is like a freak,
Fog of red, steams.

25

My People

- **BASANTH S. GOWDA** -

****

I found them now
It's suspicious. How?

My hands are held
And my flaws are loved
It feels like home
I'm never alone.

I got my people
Despite those quarrel
Memories are made
Scars easily fade.

We always giggle
And never settle
Thousand of smiles
Hundreds of words.

A fetch to my boredom
Wings of freedom

They are my people
Through all tangle.

They are my friends
No matter what's the end
I've found them now
It's suspicious. How?

26

Mental Health

- **ADITYA MAURYA** -

****

Why does no one speak?
Why do people don't care?
One is fighting inside his own,
But see the world never bother.

Are we human?
This question arises.
Leaving someone indulged in thoughts,
We just ask "Are you fine?"

Let's make it clear
Let them speak.
Show them the pyre
Of what we feel.

Don't stop yourself in backspace
Let's talk about mental health,
Tell your problems,
Scream out of your heart loud.

Let's make this world beautiful again
By not hiding one hidden side.
Let's smile let's cry
Throw out the evil and live life.
Let's say "No to Suicide"

27

The Bottle

- DEEPAK GOUD -

****

Sometimes people drink, to forget a name
After a few glasses and roses come to the bottle of wine
The only thing that comes to my mind and you were only mine
And it sticks with me through every night.

No matter what the world thinks you are pure and divine
Like the stars in the sky everywhere you shine
It's just you and me dreaming of us being on the same line
If you ever think about true love your gonna look behind
Even if I'm on my deathbed I will be waiting for your sign.

The bottle of wine is the life in the rear
Brings the past life into gear
My soul is bleeding with eyes in tears
Please help me get this night out of fear.

28

Live Your Life to the Fullest

- N. R. SANJAY KUMAR -

****

Live life as you wish
Live the way you want to leave
More with joy and happiness
Less with sorrow and sadness.

No one is permanent
No one is temporary
Be yourself with self esteem
Be yourself with honour.

Failure is not permanent,
Success is not temporary
Try your best to be the best
My friend, strive to be a LEGEND!

Learn to be different
Learn to be unique
Learn to be friendly
Learn to discover and invent.

Love is a special feeling,
Can only be felt by the heart
Affection, care, and deep tenderness
Always trusts, hopes, and perseveres
Love never fails to succeed!

Birth is the start
Death is the end
Life is very short, my friend
So, always be happy!

29

The Prophet Hen

- EASHAN SAJU -

****

As day broke out in Leeds,
Hysteria erupted at the sect.
As there is an egg in the chicken feed,
That said,' Christ is to Resurrect'.
Three eggs on display
Near where Mary's hen tended.
While there were buffoons who cried with dismay,
'The end is nigh, days numbered,
Our way of life soon upended.'
Other loons babbled
'Hurray, the lord will arrive,
Salvation for all our lives.'
While the rest remain addled.
Then a year had past
And no sights of the Lord, alas
As the populace confused
Now knew the ruse
As the eggs were written with acid.

30

Woman

- PRIYANSHEE MISHRA -

****

Her smile was too big
Her laugh was too loud
She was always too happy
And that's when I started to doubt.

The smallest thing that caught my eyes
Like biting nails and long sighs,
And yet she was the brightest star
Hiding away all the pain and scars.

There were times when she wanted to scream
To be left all alone was all that she could wish
But she was always reminded that tears are for the weak
And as a woman, crying was vulnerability at its peak.

31

The Stronger 'Me'

- VARSHINI H. R -

****

I cry myself to sleep at night
Wondering what I did wrong
And as I hug my pillow tight
I think why we can't get along.

I'm sorry you can't accept me
For whom I am inside
I'm sorry for your cruel words
Make me want to hide

You call me names like ugly and fat
How do you think I'll live with that?
How much longer could I take it?
Constantly trying not to break?

Don't you see what you put me through,
When I did you nothing wrong?
You seem to think that I am weak
But all of this has made me strong.

32

The 'Me' in 'Me'

-SHASHANK SHEKHAR RAI -

****

Many artists write poems on what they see,
Like nature, people, sky;
But I just wanted write poem about me,
I know well, I'm not a poet but the least I can do a try.

I'm someone who is not smart but,
I'm someone whom you would like,
I'm someone whom you could give your heart,
I'm someone who behave like a child.

When people are around, I become shy,
When my friends are around, I'm on the clouds.

I'm just a normal guy
Of all dreams of my own
And a family waiting to get proud of me.

33

In Harmony With Our Own Existence

- CHANDRA BHUSAN KUMAR YADAV -

****

The more I accept myself as I am,
The more weightlessness I feel.

Harmony and existence come into being,
When I am myself.

Crisis brings strength into me,
When I flow with crisis.

Seeing things as they are,
Freedom come into me.

Freedom from my discriminating mind,
Brings harmony to everyone.

Harmony brings happiness,
When I feel liberated from the world.

34

Mystery

- SINDHU R. -

****

Her life was a book of mystery
Covered with dust, unread, unheard.
Of the eyes she met
And the paths she passed
Her stories were read by them
But none read it till the end.

She wrote about everyone she met,
Hoping someone would write about her.
She always sat in the corner
Hoping for someone to hear
But no ever did.
Her story always remained a
Mystery.

Now when she is gone
Her story remains unsaid
They search her in every other book
But she has never been found.

35

Sister

- AYUSH KUMAR -

****

Doing meaningless quarrels and annoying fights,
We grew up together like two stars shining bright,
We are opposite like the colour black and white,
But in combination we fit together perfectly right.

You're screaming and complaining on each silly act,
And the poor me being scolded as daddy got your back,
And you used to even up things by sharing chocolates,
But soon we were again back to normal fighting like cats.

You helped me to heal whenever I got scratches or injury,
You offered me your share of food whenever I got hungry,
Your love didn't come with terms, conditions and expiry,
That's why I say sisters are the most precious jewellery.

36

Wine, My Ergotamine

- **KIRAN KUMAR Y. S** -

****

Girl, I saw you when I was nine
So I made you mine
I know are divine
When I told it on valentine
You showed the guy in the frontline
I know you like his hairline
But it didn't feel right.
You were the one in my wildest dreams.

Soon,
It made me confine
So, I loved cocaine
This is how you made me shine
Today, I was little high on wine
It made me forget the next line.

But, It's Fine!

37

Colour Blind

- SHARVARI P. -

****

I feel black when I think of the things that I lack
I feel pink when you wink
I feel white when things are going just right
I feel gray when I have a gloomy day
I feel yellow when it's mellow
I feel red when you text him first instead
I feel blue when I realise how you are faithful and true
I feel green when I think of home
I feel rainbow when I see myself grow
And I feel colour blind when I lose myself and I lose my mind.

38

Inevitable Destiny

- V. MOKSHITH -

****

A rockstar in Los Angeles, mapping his world tours
A homemaker in Munich busy with her chores
A top ranked Indian minister weighing his opponent
All, but all, were not spared by it
Hopes and ambitions rule over our lives
Tears and smiles are part and parcel of it
Truth, lies, influence our lives
All, but all, were not spared by it
All, but all, were not spared by covid
Families shattered; friends lost
Life, sweet life sprayed away like dust
Darkness and boring, the year became morbid.
Once again, we learnt how inevitable destiny is.
Rich, poor, famous, all became ordinary.
All but mortals, fragile mortals
Covid thought us to live with what is just necessary.

39

Voice of Failure

- **PRINCE GUPTA** -

****

"You are a failure, that's what they call you, isn't it?"
My mind questioned.

It left me in dismay,
I had never dealt with anything
More difficult than my own soul.

It's not aways your cup of tea
That everything goes in your foresight direction.

Yet it doesn't mean I am a failure,
Still that's what they call me.
I was trying to fight with my thoughts and peace.

Stop it!
It's useless to make efforts when you can't change things.
"You've been a looser"
My mind was harsh on me.

"I know I can do better,

Failure is a positive opportunity to learn and grow.
I don't take it as a negative experience
Or it will hinder my success",
I tried to convince myself.

Printed by Libri Plureos GmbH in Hamburg,
Germany